Cursive Writing Practice
Inspiring Quotes

Jane Lierman

NEW YORK • TORONTO • LONDON • AUCKLAND • SYDNEY
MEXICO CITY • NEW DELHI • HONG KONG • BUENOS AIRES

Teaching *Resources*

*Dedicated to those who inspire others
through their ideas, words, art, and actions.*

A special thanks to Norm Brauer, Kemy Lin, Robert Alemán,
and Sarah Longhi who inspired the creation of this book.

Scholastic Inc. grants teachers permission to photocopy the reproducible pages from this book for classroom use. No other
part of this publication may be reproduced in whole or in part, or stored in a retrieval system, or transmitted in any form or
by any means, electronic, mechanical, photocopying, recording, or otherwise, without written permission of the publisher.
For information regarding permission, write to Scholastic Inc., 557 Broadway, New York, NY 10012.

Edited by Sarah Longhi

Cover design by Maria Lilja
Interior design and illustrations by Robert Alemán Design
Illustrations by Kemy Lin, pages 21-23, 25-26, 39, and 41.

ISBN-13: 978-0-545-09437-5
ISBN-10: 0-545-09437-2

Copyright © 2008 by Jane Lierman.
All rights reserved.
Printed in the U.S.A.
14 15 16   40   19 18 17

Contents

Introduction

A favorite classroom routine from my own school days was copying an inspiring quote from the board before history class began. Our history teacher regularly presented us with quotes from famous people to set the tone for the class, stimulate thinking, and encourage discussion. The same routine continues with my students when we work on cursive writing; I have students copy a meaningful quote to practice good penmanship and presentation, and then I use it as a tool for building relationships, inspiring creative thinking, and especially encouraging positive actions.

Purpose

Cursive Writing Practice: Inspiring Quotes provides students with a purposeful activity to reinforce cursive skills and quality work. This collection of quotes helps you generate rich discussions about key character-building traits, such as kindness and determination—and familiarize students with important role models, such as Gandhi, Eleanor Roosevelt, and Martin Luther King, Jr. To underscore the importance of writing effectively and legibly, you may want to have students compile their collection of inspirational quotes—written in their neatest handwriting—in a keepsake quote book, described below.

How to Use This Book

You may simply have students practice copying the quotes as an individual or center activity, or you may guide the whole class to make a keepsake quote book, as explained in the procedure on the next page. In either case, be sure to introduce and discuss the quotes before students begin to work on the practice pages.

- Tell students that many of the words and phrases that inspire us come from people of various cultures throughout history. The words become memorable quotes when they cause us to think and move us to positive actions.

- Share a few of the quotes from this book that are meaningful to you as a teacher; ask students to share a memorable saying or quote that they have heard.

- Add that the second purpose of the book is to practice the skill of writing legibly. Encourage them to analyze their own writing and focus on one of four areas to improve:

  - Letter formation
  - Sizing of letters
  - Alignment on line
  - Spacing between letters and words

Making a Keepsake Quote Mini-Book

If you plan to have students create a keepsake mini-book of these quotes, tell them that as they practice, they will be collecting and organizing the quotes to create a booklet that they can reread and share with friends and family this year and in years to come. I always show students a finished spiral-bound version of the mini-book, which motivates them to plan for their own project and to maintain a high standard for their handwriting as they copy each quote.

Procedure

1. One or two times a week, as students arrive at school, display on the board or projector one of the quote pages. Hand out student copies of the page, as well.

2. Discuss the quote and let students share connections they may make to their lives and to literature they've read. (Option: If the quote is directly connected to a school situation or historical event, you might require students to memorize the quote.)

3. Check students' work for legibility.

4. Tell students to cut off the bottom section of the page along the dashed line and initial the back of the page.

5. Have students save the finished quotes in an envelope or file folder until all the quotes are completed.

6. At the end of the year, have each student put the set of pages in an order that is meaningful to him or her.

7. For the front and back covers, have students decorate and cut sturdy paper to size (approximately 4 x 11 inch). Staple the mini-book along the left edge. (Option: For the covers use student-created art paper, such as marbled paper.) To create a very sturdy cover, cut to size two laminated pieces of construction paper per student. Add labels for the title and the byline. Spiral-bind or staple together the pages and covers.

8. Send home the completed quote mini-book at the end of the year as an inspirational keepsake.

Paper-Saving Option

Recycled Paper Mini-Book

1. Create a blank spiral-bound mini-book with sturdy covers and 40 blank pages from recycled paper. (To conserve paper, use a half piece of paper for each mini-book page.)

2. Copy and laminate an alphabet sample from page 47 for each student or group of students.

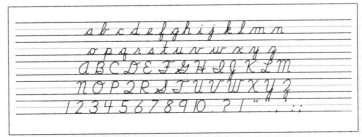

3. Copy and laminate a lined template for each student from page 48. Store books, laminated alphabets, and laminated templates in a plastic tub for safekeeping. (These tools can be reused with future classes.)

4. Show the quote on the screen or write it on the board and have students copy it in their premade blank mini-book, using the lined template under the blank page as a guide for correct spacing. (You may want to have them first practice writing the quote in a notebook before making a final copy in their quote book.)

5. Students may draw illustrations or cut and paste pictures into their book.

6. Send the completed quote book home as a keepsake at the end of the year.

Attitude

Name _____

Date _____

Attitudes are contagious! Is yours worth catching?

—Author Unknown

Practice these words.

Attitudes

are

worth

Use your best handwriting to copy the quote below.

✂

Attitude

7

Name

Date

Considering all of the things you wear, your expression is the most important.

–Janet Lane (1877–1967)

Practice these words.

Considering

wear

expression

Use your best handwriting to copy the quote below.

✂

Name _____

Date _____

Practice an attitude of gratitude.

—Author Unknown

Practice these words.

Practice

of

gratitude

Use your best handwriting to copy the quote below.

9

Attitude

Name _____

Date _____

A pessimist sees the difficulty in every opportunity;
an optimist sees the opportunity in every difficulty.

—Winston Churchill (1874–1965)

Practice these words.

every

opportunity

optimist

Use your best handwriting to copy the quote below.

✂

Winston Churchill

Attitude

Name _____

Date _____

An optimist sees the doughnut. A pessimist sees the hole.

—Elaine McLaundburgh Wilson

Practice these words.

optimist

doughnut

pessimist

Use your best handwriting to copy the quote below.

Attitude

Name _____

Date _____

Character isn't inherited. One builds it daily by the way
one thinks and acts, thought by thought, action by action.
—Helen Douglas (1900–1980)

Practice these words.

Character

isn't

inherited

Use your best handwriting to copy the quote below.